The Flying Fox Warriors

Introduction

On one level, The Flying Fox Warriors *relates the story of the origin of the bats and birds. On another, however, we may have an account of a clash between two different Australian peoples, the Robust (the Flying Fox People) and the Gracile (the Bird People). Archaeologists believe the Robust, also known as Java Man, first arrived in Australia at least 130,000 years ago; the Gracile arrived about 60,000 years later. According to Aboriginal oral tradition, these two peoples once clashed long ago. The tale of* The Flying Fox Warriors, *however, mythologizes the incident and places the tale in Aboriginal Dreamtime.*

The myths of the Aboriginal people spring from a time long ago when human beings were the only living creatures on Earth. The first human beings, who came from the stars, possessed supernatural powers. These ancestral beings brought the world into existence, creating the land and the sea. They brought knowledge, morality, and law. Life on Earth was good in that ancient time until cataclysmic changes rocked the land. Disaster came to Earth in the form of floods, volcanoes, droughts, and earthquakes. Fear moved many of the first ancestors to seek refuge in a most remarkable way. They transformed themselves into animals, birds, plants, insects — and even rocks — as they attempted to hide and protect themselves. It was during this tumultuous time of transition that Dreamtime commenced and the Earth came to be populated with the multitude of life forms we know today.

Dick Roughsey, co-author and illustrator, was an Aboriginal man born on the island of Langu-narnji in the Gulf of Carpentaria. His Aboriginal name was Goobalathaldin. For 25 years, until his death, he and his collaborator, Percy Trezise, worked to preserve the lore of these Stone Age people of Australia. Trezise was privileged to be admitted to the inner, secret and sacred circle of Aboriginal life in 1974. This has special significance, for the Aboriginals guard their lore and will share its complexity only with the initiated. Trezise continues to document the tales he learned through his friendship with Roughsey, both in paintings and through the written word.

Library of Congress Cataloging-in-Publication Data

Trezise, Percy and Roughsey, Dick.
  The flying fox warriors.

  (Stories of the dreamtime — tales of the Aboriginal people)
  Summary: A battle to the death between two enemy tribes in the
Dreamtime leads to the appearance of the bats known as flying foxes
and subsequently to the rise of all kinds of birds.
    [1. Australian –aborigines—Legends. 2. Flying foxes—Folklore. 3. Bats—
Folklore. 4. Birds—Folklore] I. Trezise, Percy, ill. II. Roughsey, Dick, ill. III. Title.
IV. Series: Stories of the dreamtime.
PA8.1.T72F1   1988   398.2'452'0994   [E]   88-20123
ISBN 1-55532-946-2 (lib. bdg.)

North American edition first published in 1988 by

Gareth Stevens, Inc.
7317 West Green Tree Road
Milwaukee, WI 53223 USA

First published in Australia by William Collins Pty. Ltd.

Editor: Kathy Keller
Introduction: Kathy Keller
Map: Mario Macari
Design: Kate Kriege

1 2 3 4 5 6 7 8 9 9 92 91 90 89 88

The Flying Fox Warriors

story and art by

PERCY TREZISE & DICK ROUGHSEY

Gareth Stevens Publishing
Milwaukee

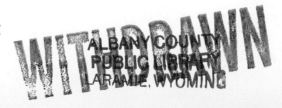

Long, long ago in Dreamtime, when many living creatures were still in human form, the Bird people were troubled by the Flying Fox people, called the Joonging.

The Joonging had many young warriors who raided the camps of the Bird people and stole their young women for wives. One morning they wounded Goorangi, the Emu, one of the Bird people's strongest warriors.

As the Bird men helped pull the spears out of him, Goorangi said angrily, "We must stop the Joonging men from stealing our young women. Call all the clans together. We must decide what to do."

Young Bird warriors ran off in all directions, heading for the camps of the Brolgas, Cockatoos, Kookaburras, Banana Birds, Parrots, Crows, Geese, Jabirus, Rainbow Lorikeets, and others.

It took five days for all the Bird people to gather. The great warriors of each clan stood on large rocks. Each one said what he thought they should do about the Joonging.

Goorangi, the Emu, spoke last. "As they steal our women, their
clans grow large and strong, while ours grow small and weak.
Tomorrow we will send out our scouts to find their main camp,"
said Goorangi.

In the pale light of early dawn the bands of young scouts gathered up their weapons and prepared to travel in all directions to find the Flying Fox camp.

The Bil-bil brothers said to the Crow and Cockatoo brothers, "We will travel east, toward the sunrise. There we have seen many tracks of Joonging warriors along a river that flows out of a great mountain range."

After traveling two days, running from dawn to dark, they reached the big river. The Crow brothers soon found tracks of a large band of Joonging warriors going upstream. They also found the tracks of two young girls.

The Bil-bils said, "It is a raiding party of Joonging. They have captured two Sea Gull girls and are returning to camp. We will follow at a distance and trail them to their camp."

The Bird scouts tracked the Joonging for three days. The river they were following became smaller as they traveled upstream climbing into the high, rugged mountains.

On the third evening, just after sunset, they saw the Joonging cross over the last high ridge and disappear down the other side. They decided to camp below and cross the ridge at night, when they would be hidden by darkness.

Next morning, just before sunrise, they topped the rocky ridge and saw the most awesome sight. Just below them, on a wide, grassy plain, was the main camp of the Joonging people.

16

The camp stretched as far as the eye could see, with people everywhere. Some slept beside fires or in wurlies. Others sat or walked, while some practiced fighting with spears, boomerangs, and nulla-nullas.

17

Suddenly, without warning, there was a hiss and a thud as a Flying Fox spear struck one of the Crow brothers. Ferociously the Flying Fox attacked the enemy Bird scouts, who fought desperately for their lives.

18

The Bil-bil brothers stood back to back, using their nulla-nullas to fend off spears and boomerangs, cracking the heads and limbs of their attackers.

The Bird scouts beat off the Joonging, then picked up the wounded Crow scout. The Bil-bils ran into a cave which none of them knew was the home of evil Turramulli, the Giant Quinkin.

Inside they could hardly see each other and held hands to keep together. None knew that the hand which led them belonged to a friendly Timara Quinkin, who sneaked them past snoring Turramulli, to another way out at the other side of the mountain.

When the Bil-bils reached home two days later, there was another meeting of all the Bird clans. Goorangi and the other big warriors listened to the Bil-bil brothers as they described the vast Flying Fox camp.

When they finished, Goorangi said, "We do not have enough fighting men to conquer them, so we must try to surround them with a terrible fire and burn them."

Early one hot, dry summer morning, the Bird warriors crept up on the Flying Fox camp. As the sun began to rise, the Bird warriors used firesticks to light a ring of fire around the camp.

24

The Joonging people saw that they were trapped. Some tried to run through the fire. There was a terrible confusion as they fell over each other in two big heaps where most of them were burned.

As the fire died down, the few Joonging people who remained changed themselves into flying foxes and formed a new clan. With wings, they would never again be caught by bush fires.

The two huge heaps of burned bodies turned to stone, and were named Kalkajagga. Today they are known as the Black Mountains near Cooktown.

Waga the Crow watched the flying Joonging. "How wonderful it would be to fly over the hills," he cried. "Let us also change into birds, all kinds of birds."

Goorangi started to change into an Emu, but his wings wouldn't grow. He said to Cassowary, who had the same problem, "We won't need wings. We are big and strong and can run fast!"

And so today, Cassowary and Emu cannot fly, but are happy as they run about. All the birds take little notice of the Joonging as they fly overhead after sunset, even though once more their population is vast.

While the birds feed on fruit and blossoms during the day, the flying foxes wait for the nighttime to feed. Enemies long ago in Dreamtime, the flying foxes now live peacefully in the same land with the multitude of birds.

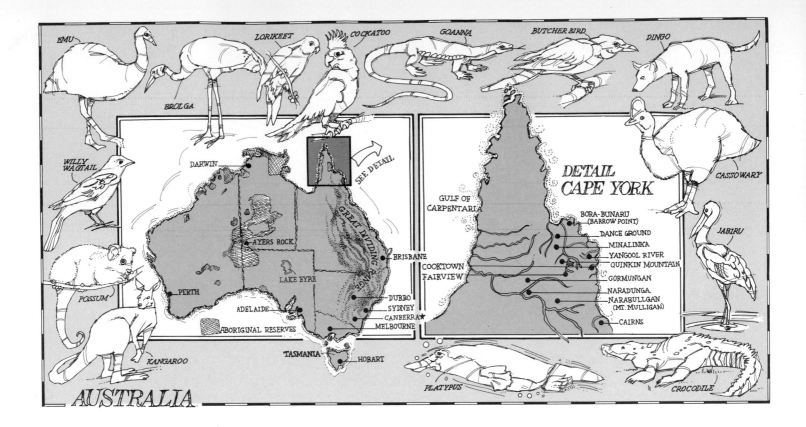

Glossary

bil-bil (BILL bill): a Rainbow Lorikeet, which is a brightly colored Australian parrot

brolga (BROL gah): a large silver-gray bird which performs an exotic courtship dance

cassowary (CASS o ware ee): a large Australian bird that looks something like an ostrich

clan: a group of families claiming a common ancestor

Dreamtime: the time long ago in Aboriginal mythology when supernatural ancestors created the world

emu (E myu): a three-toed, flightless bird related to the ostrich

fend: to ward off, to push away in defense

firestick: a burning stick used to start fires

flying fox: a large Australian bat with a fox-like face

Goorangi (goo RAHN jee): the emu, a warrior of the Bird people

jabiru (ja bi RU): an Australian stork

Joonging (JOON ging): an Aboriginal people also known as the Flying Fox people

Kalkajagga (kahl kah JAHG gah): the Black Mountains near Cooktown in northeastern Australia

lorikeet (LOR ih keet): a brightly colored Australian parrot

nulla-nulla (null lah NULL lah): an Aboriginal club used as a weapon

Quinkin (KWIN kin): a type of Aboriginal spirit who roamed the bushland

Timara (tih MAH rah): a good Quinkin

Turramulli (toor ah MULL lee): the evil, giant Quinkin

Waga (WAH gah): the crow, a warrior of the Bird people

wurlies (WUHR leez): Aboriginal huts or shelters made of boughs, leaves, and grass

32